D0289282

THE
TO-BE
LIST

Blue Mountain Arts®

New and Best-Selling Titles

By Susan Polis Schutz:
To My Daughter with Love on the Important Things in Life
To My Grandchild with Love
To My Son with Love

By Douglas Pagels:
Always Remember How Special You Are to Me
Required Reading for All Teenagers
The Next Chapter of Your Life
You Are One Amazing Lady

By Marci:
Friends Are Forever
10 Simple Things to Remember
To My Daughter
To My Granddaughter
To My Mother
To My Sister
To My Son
You Are My "Once in a Lifetime"

By Wally Amos, with Stu Glauberman:
The Path to Success Is Paved with Positive Thinking

By Minx Boren:
Friendship Is a Journey
Healing Is a Journey

By Debra DiPietro:
Short Morning Prayers

Anthologies:
A Daybook of Positive Thinking
A Son Is Life's Greatest Gift
Dream Big, Stay Positive, and Believe in Yourself
God Is Always Watching Over You
Hang In There
The Love Between a Mother and Daughter Is Forever
Nothing Fills the Heart with Joy like a Grandson
There Is Nothing Sweeter in Life Than a Granddaughter
There Is So Much to Love About You... Daughter
Think Positive Thoughts Every Day
Words Every Woman Should Remember
You Are Stronger Than You Know

THE
TO-BE
LIST

70 REMINDERS THAT LIFE IS
ABOUT BEING, NOT DOING

Latesha Randall WITH *Sebastian Walter*

Blue Mountain Press™
Boulder, Colorado

Copyright © 2017 by Latesha Randall.
Copyright © 2017 by Blue Mountain Arts, Inc.

All rights reserved. No part of this publication may be reproduced, stored in a retrieval system or transmitted in any form or by any means, electronic, mechanical, photocopying, recording or otherwise, without the written permission of the publisher.

Library of Congress Cataloging-in-Publication data is available upon request.
ISBN: 978-1-68088-129-5

◼ and Blue Mountain Press are registered in U.S. Patent and Trademark Office.
Certain trademarks are used under license.

Printed in China.
Second Printing: 2017

♻ This book is printed on recycled paper.

This book is printed on paper that has been specially produced to be acid free (neutral pH) and contains no groundwood or unbleached pulp. It conforms with the requirements of the American National Standards Institute, Inc., so as to ensure that this book will last and be enjoyed by future generations.

Blue Mountain Arts, Inc.

P.O. Box 4549, Boulder, Colorado 80306

Contents

Welcome to *The To-Be List*

This list was created for people like you—smart, busy, ambitious, driven, goal-setting go-getters who amaze friends and family with how much they manage to accomplish at work, at home, or wherever they are! Like them, you are a truly incredible human, but most of the time—if you're honest with yourself—you feel like a human *doing*, not a human *being.* You feel as if there are never enough hours in the day, you can never possibly check everything off your to-do list, and you'll never be good enough or able to do enough.

Sometimes you just want someone to give you a little perspective and remind you that life isn't all about doing—it's about the beautiful journey of *becoming.* That's exactly what *The To-Be List* is: short, thoughtful, inspiring reflections on things to *be*—character qualities to adopt, values to ponder, and parts of your soul to reignite. We encourage you to read one section of this book a day. This is not a mission to power through all in one go so you can check it off and say "Done!" Enjoy it slowly from the comfort of a special snuggly spot with a cup of tea or piece of chocolate. This is a book to savor and think on daily.

Here's to your journey of transforming from a human doing to a human being. We invite you to cherish every single minute of it!

—Tesh & Seb

Be Present

How many times have you found yourself listening to a friend—nodding in agreement with what they're saying—while mentally planning out your evening, remembering an item you need to pick up on the way home, or reliving something you said earlier?

We seem to find ourselves living in the past or future far more than we're ever really in the present, and it becomes almost impossible for us to truly be there for others, even those we care deeply about. Meanwhile we're missing out on relationships… and we're missing out on life.

As life unfolds around us, we're either days behind or weeks ahead playing over moments that have been or longing for ones in the future. In reality, neither of those actually exist. The only truly real moment is the one you're experiencing right now.

Try, just for one day, being present. Push away those nagging thoughts that want to distract you from where you *actually are*, who you're *really with*, and what is happening *right in front of you*. Give others your full attention—not a tiny fraction of it—and watch what happens inside you and around you. Suddenly life may start to become more interesting, more beautiful, and more appreciated. *Be present.*

Be
Perseverant

I'm watching a spider hard at work creating a masterpiece behind the bedroom door. I've just opened my eyes after sleep and observe from my bed as the fine, silvery strands are woven—stretching from the door to the wall. I admire her work, but I have information she doesn't: soon I'm going to get up and open the bedroom door to begin my day. And due to an unfortunate choice of location, this webby masterpiece will be destroyed.

I lie there pondering the spider's reaction to this sort of unexpected setback. Then it clicks—*there won't be one.* The spider won't shake her spindly legs in fury, cursing the gods and her bad luck. She won't fall into a deep despondency, relying on comfort food and mind-numbing movies to ease her loss. Instead, she's going to wander over to another corner of the room and start again.

It's the same with everything you observe in nature—ants keep marching, trees keep finding a route to the sun, and moss continues slowly growing over rocks until it creates a carpet of green.

Remember that spider next time life throws you a curve ball. If the spot you've chosen to build a web doesn't work out, simply pick a different one and keep right on building. *Be perseverant.*

Be
Slow

'm betting you are cringing just reading those two words. Images of snails and sloths arise from your subconscious storage space.

Slow? What's good about being slow? A fair question. In today's world, slow = lazy. Slow = incompetent. Slow = less effective. All these thoughts run through my mind as I try to drag my dawdling puppy along for our walk. "Hurry up!" I demand, glancing at my watch for the fourth time. I have things to do. Lachie, however, is blissfully unaware of this, begging me to stop and pay attention to the oh-so-sniffable leaf he's found.

I often forget the joys of slowing down. Even a walk with my puppy is a race against the clock—just another item to get ticked off the list. But little by little, I'm starting to take life at a slower pace. Maybe you'd like to try as well.

Here are a few "slow experiments" to start with:

- *Eat slowly.* Savor each mouthful instead of wolfing down your food, anxious to move on to dessert and then to doing the dishes, and then... you know how it goes. Instead, chew, savor, swallow, and enjoy.

- *Breathe slowly.* We often take hurried, shallow breaths, which don't allow enough oxygen to circulate effectively. Allow yourself the privilege of inhaling and exhaling slowly throughout the day.

- *Walk slowly.* Lengthen your stride and look around as you walk. Take in the smells, sights, and sounds. You'll arrive at your destination feeling a lot less flustered and have heaps more fun getting there!

Sometimes fast isn't all it's cracked up to be. Try slow on for size; you just might like it. *Be slow.*

Be
Teachable

Working as a writer with other writers, I've noticed the curious phenomenon of typos: we spot everyone else's but often fail to see our own. When we've been staring at a piece of copy for hours... tweaking, changing, and editing, it's easy to become oblivious to our mistakes. The content reads perfectly to us—after all, we know exactly what it is that we're trying to say. Pass it on to a fresh pair of eyes, however, and we get a whole new perspective. Others can see what we have missed.

Is it possible to apply the same concept to our lives?

We get so busy doing what we do the way we know how to do it that our self-imposed blinders block out areas we might need to change. So when someone comes along and says, "Have you ever thought about trying this?" or "Perhaps you could have handled that situation better," our natural reaction is to get defensive. "How dare they criticize me. They don't know what they're talking about!" I know that's been my response many times in my own life.

I'm working to become more teachable, welcome suggestions, invite further comments, and appreciate that perhaps the people in my life can sometimes see my "typos" better than I can. Perhaps you would like to join me? Together, we can learn to *be teachable*.

Be
Adventurous

It's a big world out there. When was the last time you stepped off your familiar route and into the unknown?

Adventure doesn't have to mean bungee jumping or skydiving from a plane at 15,000 feet (although this certainly gets your heart pumping!). It could simply be checking out the park down the road—the one you drive past every day and think, "That looks like a nice place to go for a walk. I really should go there sometime." Or it could be going into that food store you often walk straight past and buying some new spices to try out.

Maybe you could wear that shirt you didn't think you'd be able to pull off or try a different meal at the restaurant where you usually order the same dish. You could sign up for a class that looks challenging, outside your comfort zone, and FULL of adventure!

We're only here on this earth for a short time. Let's not spend it all doing the same routine things. Instead, let's *be adventurous.*

Be a
Self-Encourager

It would be nice if everyone out there were ready to give you a pat on the back when you need it. But sometimes even the best friends are too busy with their own problems to realize when a word of encouragement would really help. That's okay, though, because you know who is always around? YOU! And it's surprisingly easy and effective to become your own encourager.

The secret is to move beyond just thinking positive things (which is great!) to *verbalizing* those things throughout the day (which is even better!).

Yes, that means talking out loud. To yourself. Like a crazy person. But, hey, who first decided that was crazy anyway? Speaking out loud brings clarity. It gives a sense of purpose to your words, taking them beyond the "invisible" world of thought to an audible reality. I personally love motivating myself during the day. I'll celebrate out loud when something goes well ("Oh awesome! This is so exciting!"), and I'll tell myself it's okay when things aren't going so smoothly ("The day is bound to get better. You've got this!").

I've found that with practice, I can shift my mood in a matter of seconds. Whereas previously I might have been trapped in a negative thought spiral of worry, now I can snap out of that by just talking to myself.

It might seem weird. And yes, people may look at you a little funny if they happen to be passing by while you're having a self-pep-talk, but if it works, who cares? There's no need to wait around feeling glum, hoping someone will come along and say something nice to you. Do it yourself! Use positive words to change your attitude. See it as the path to sanity. *Be a self-encourager.*

Be
Restrained

It's tempting you—all dark, chocolaty, and irresistible. That cake is crying out to be eaten, and you're listening. You know just how much you deserve to have a big slice—never mind that you've already had a slice today. After all, you're *entitled*. You work hard. You *need* to treat yourself. I know those excuses. I've eaten that cake. But I've recently discovered that restraint can be amazingly freeing.

For years I lived by an "if it's there, it should be eaten" policy. But who was I eating it for? Not for my body, which couldn't do anything useful with it. Not for my taste buds, which would only enjoy it for a second. Nope, I was just eating it for the same reason that most of us do what we don't need to… *because I could.*

There's a strange pleasure in saying *no*—in knowing you can trust yourself and honor your body. Whether it's alcohol, relationships, food, television, or the Internet, you know the areas of your life where restraint seems to conveniently go on holiday. Invite restraint back home. Ask it to move in, unpack its bags, and stay for the long haul. Say to that slice of cake, "Go sweet-talk someone else. I can *be restrained*."

Be
Selfless

I asked a friend what selflessness means, and he told me an ancient Buddhist parable of how a boar once heard the cries of a starving lioness that was unable to feed her cubs, and so he gave himself to them for food. This extreme act horrified me at first, but I realized that this same story has been played out by great leaders who were willing to lay down everything for others throughout history.

Selflessness goes beyond a random act of generosity.

To be selfless is to take yourself out of the equation… to forget yourself completely and cast off any of your own conceived importance in favor of the bigger picture.

Can you do that? It can be easy enough in certain moments, like when the people you care about require more love than you thought you had to give. But to live a selfless life daily… that's a real challenge. Are you prepared to take it? Can you make the dreams of others more important than your own? Can you place their needs higher on your priority list? You have the power to make the decision every day to *be selfless*.

Be
Childlike

Close your eyes for a second and try to recall what it was like to be five years old. Remember being small and free from work, responsibility, and pressure? We often look back on our younger years and think, "Ah, how far I've come! How much wiser, smarter, and more important I am now than I was then!" But I think there are plenty of lessons for us to learn from our five-year-old selves.

Children are:

* *Charmingly friendly.* Do you smile at strangers all the time just for fun? Children do.

* *Incredibly open.* You only have to know a child for two seconds to hear their deepest secrets, greatest loves, and biggest fears. We worldly-wise adults can take years to open up to the people we consider closest to us!

* *Constantly questioning.* Why? How come? What's that? Children understand that the best way to learn is by asking questions. So they just let 'em flow.

🌸 *Always exploring.* Do you have a big tree, a high staircase, or a propped-up ladder? You better believe a child would be climbing up them before you could turn around! Children don't hesitate to get out there and see what there is to see.

🌸 *Unbelievably resilient.* Perhaps this is the natural result of all the tree climbing and consequent falling, but have you noticed how children seem to handle some of life's hardest knocks with grace and ease? Divorce, pain, death, tragedy, criticism... somehow, even at their tender age, kids are able to pull through and keep on going.

So give your younger self some credit—you had a lot going for you, and you still do! It's all tucked away inside you, ready to be accessed when you learn to *be childlike*.

Be Receptive

What is your reaction when someone approaches you with a new idea, like a new book to read, a link to an online article, an invitation to an event, or thoughts on one of your closely held beliefs?

Do you say, "Thanks, but I already have my own _____, follow my own _____, know all about _____."? Or perhaps you drop the thanks altogether and go straight into defense mode: "I don't know why you'd think I'd be interested in that." These reactions are pretty standard—I've heard them come out of my own mouth many times.

It's only since adopting a new response that my horizons have started to broaden. It goes like this: "Wow! Thanks for taking the time to send me _____, give me _____, invite me to _____. I'll definitely check it out and let you know my thoughts." This receptive approach expresses interest, shows appreciation for the other person's time and effort, and opens you up to new possibilities.

It's very easy to be closed off—and most of us are to more things than we're aware of. It's challenging but so much more rewarding to *be receptive.*

Be
Vulnerable
by Seb

Many of us try to avoid getting hurt emotionally or physically. So we avoid saying "I love you" first because of the fear that we'll be rejected; we don't voice creative ideas in business meetings because we're afraid of being ridiculed by our colleagues; or we tell our friends we have it all figured out and know what we're doing next with our lives, when in fact we're a bit lost and looking for a new direction. We get defensive and closed off when our partner challenges us because we don't want to be perceived as imperfect, or we shun taking charge and being responsible because we fear we might fail. The ways we can avoid vulnerability are countless.

But research shows that accepting vulnerability is the key to feeling worthy of deep connection with our fellow human beings and ourselves. When we let down our barriers and tell our true stories with our whole heart—when we embrace the risk of being rejected, ridiculed, hurt, or heartbroken—we practice courage. We act with authenticity in order to be who we really are and let go of who we think we ought to be.

Be aware of situations where you're facing emotional risk, personal exposure, and uncertainty. Embrace these situations as opportunities to be vulnerable, and practice courage, compassion, and authenticity. You'll experience more joy and a deeper connection with your fellow human beings if you can just *be vulnerable.*

Be
Flexible

This has nothing to do with your ability (or lack thereof) to do the splits or bend over and touch your toes.

Growing up, I was inflexible. I loved having a "plan"—and heaven forbid that this plan should ever change! This caused considerable difficulties for my parents and my friends—but most of all for me. I felt stressed and anxious if life didn't work out exactly how I wanted, and that happened, well... all the time.

But when does anything ever go exactly as planned? The world and the people in it are in a constant state of flux—shifting, moving, growing, and changing. A friend might not be able to meet for coffee like you had planned. A coworker could get sick in the middle of a big project. Your "perfect match" may turn out to be not so perfect.

You can tense up and poise yourself to fight... or you can be flexible. You can bend like a deeply rooted tree in a fierce gale, move around, find a solution, change your plans—*and be okay with that.* You'll find life becomes much more enjoyable when you can *be flexible.*

Be Friendly

We're surrounded by potential friends every day. Yet most of us are so caught up in our own existing circles that we fail to recognize anyone outside of them. This means every week we're possibly missing out on hundreds of opportunities to make new, exciting connections. Even if we don't plan on becoming best buddies with every person who crosses our path, it costs us absolutely nothing to be friendly.

Here are three little tips for living a friendlier life:

- *Learn people's names.* Do you frequent certain cafés, gas stations, or supermarkets? Take notice of the person serving you, learn their name, and use it next time you go in.

- *Chat with people around you.* I've made many interesting connections on planes, buses, and in checkout lines. It doesn't take much effort to say "Hello" to the person seated next to you—plus it makes the journey more fun if they're willing to chat!

- *Smile.* Smile at people walking past you, at the person behind the counter, at your coworkers—and even at people handing out flyers on the street. When you smile, the world becomes a friendlier place.

I'm a big believer in the saying, "You can never have too many friends." You'll certainly never find out whether that's true or not unless you make the extra effort to *be friendly.*

Be
Open-Minded

In our Western culture, we like to think we are pretty open-minded. And that's true, to a certain extent, until some little something stops us in our tracks and we become aware that the doorways in our minds may not be quite as open as we thought.

There are telltale signs: You might feel uptight or outraged. You may want to argue and say, "No, it isn't like that—you're wrong." It's an internal churning that comes from challenging long-held beliefs. You might try to justify these feelings by saying, "It's just my conscience telling me this isn't right." But maybe you are confusing conscience with stubbornness and plain old unwillingness to change.

There are a lot of differing beliefs out there—a lot of skin colors, cultures, and ways of cooking an egg. If you don't want to know any way other than your own, you'll never experience the joy of seeing the world through different eyes when you choose to *be open-minded*.

Be
Engaged

This is not about wearing a diamond ring on your finger. You don't need a rock to know if you're engaged. It's there in your eyes, in your attention, and in your energy. An engaged person sees what is going on around them and wants to be part of the action.

Having a conversation with someone who is really engaged makes you come alive. It's how dreams are ignited, winning strategies are formulated, and innovation is sparked.

To do work that matters, you have to get engaged. How? Notice small details. Look directly into the eyes of the person opposite you. See every situation, project, and activity in front of you as an open door you're about to intentionally walk through. And once you enter, stay there. Don't begin formulating an exit plan before you've even gotten inside. *Be engaged.*

Be Strong

by Seb

Sometimes I wonder if modern life makes us prone to suffering when confronted with adversity. We drive to work and sit in our air-conditioned offices. We take breaks whenever we think we need them. We exercise irregularly, and when we do, we go only as hard as we are comfortable with, because we are the ones choosing the intensity and endurance.

But life's intensity is not adjustable like the resistance on a stationary bike. At times we have to deal with adversity that we don't choose. It is in those situations when being strong helps us to keep calm and protect our happiness and joy for life.

For most of us, everyday life doesn't challenge us to the limits of our mental or physical capacity. Yes, some of us consciously push ourselves in jobs, sports, or hobbies. This is great and can be beneficial, but it doesn't compare to life throwing you a challenge you haven't signed up for. Going for a lunch-break jog is simply not the same as running from a saber-toothed tiger that is eager to have *you* for lunch. It's wise to be prepared and know with confidence that you can endure whatever life throws at you.

Being strong is just another mental habit. For example, lets say Guy 1 and Guy 2 feel their legs burning on the last hundred meters of an uphill run. Their inner voices are telling them to slow down and walk a couple of steps. The fundamental difference between the two men lies in their responses. Guy 1 obeys the voice and slows down. Guy 2 does exactly the opposite and uses that last hundred meters to make himself a little tougher, more resilient, and less prone to suffering—and, therefore, happier in the long term. Guy 2 went harder because he chose *lasting happiness* over immediate comfort.

So the next time you're facing an intentional challenge or involuntary adversity, choose to see it as an opportunity to try harder despite the discomfort. You won't regret it. Choose happiness over comfort, and *be strong.*

Be Respectful

Have you ever noticed how the closer your relationship is with someone, the harder it is to be respectful? We're polite to strangers and new friends, remembering our manners and not interrupting when they speak. We acknowledge and heed their boundaries. We respect others' opinions when shared at dinner parties.

But the people closest to us—our parents, partners, siblings, best friends—often get the sharp side of our tongues. They get questioned and told that they're wrong. We don't give them their space. We sigh and roll our eyes when they tell the same old story for the hundredth time.

Respect comes from the understanding that others are separate from us. They are their own beings, entitled to freedom of thought, word, opinion, action, and values. They are not ours to change or boss around.

People can only thrive when given enough space to express themselves in the way that they want. When you treat them with respect, you're saying, "You're important, you're smart, and you're strong enough to find your own way." *Be respectful.*

Be
Consistent

You said you'd be on time, and you were... the first day. You promised you'd call every Saturday, and you did... for a month. You guaranteed that yes, of course you were good for the repayments... and two deposits later the money stopped coming through.

Words are cheap. Actions accrue value.

Our reputation isn't based on how good we are at making promises; it's dependent on whether or not those promises are carried through.

We all know people who can show a flash of brilliance and make lofty promises one day, and then they disappear the next. Don't be one of them. Show up, keep your promises, and mean what you say, day after day after day after... you get the idea. *Be consistent.*

Be
Patient
by Seb

I decided to learn the guitar because I wanted to play my favorite songs and entertain my friends. When I realized that it would take a tedious year of practicing notes and chords repeatedly to get to the point of actually being able to play songs, my motivation took a hit. I got frustrated and stopped practicing.

What I lacked was patience. Patience is your ability to persist under difficult circumstances; it's the level of endurance you can take before negativity boils up.

You need patience to learn anything that is difficult at first. You were patient when you first started to walk, when you started the new job you now love, and when you learned a new hobby that now brings you so much joy.

You need patience to find your passion. There is no other way to love what you do than to fully accept the difficulties along the way. Don't distract yourself with looking to those who have progressed further along the learning curve. The only difference between you and them is time.

The next time you commit to learning something new, be aware of the difficulties that will arise along the way and decide to be gentle with yourself when frustration boils up. Let go of any expectations and enjoy the process without thinking of your desired outcome. As Michelangelo said, "Genius is eternal patience." Decide to *be patient*.

Be Frugal

Frugality is a word that makes the advertising industry recoil in distaste. Frugality conflicts with our shop till we drop, bigger is better, keeping up appearances, owning the latest gadgets, dining out, entertain me mentality. But under our designer clothing, our hearts harbor an inkling that there must be more to life than large mortgages, fast cars, credit card debt, and retail therapy.

If we could learn how to put instant gratification on hold and set money aside instead, I wonder what we could accomplish.

It's amazing how even the little things add up: two coffees a week, a few trips to the movies each month—you do the math.

If we want to change the world, achieve goals, and leave a legacy… maybe we need to recognize that sometimes doing without means we end up being able to do more. *Be frugal.*

Be Okay with Not Being Okay

All the positive self-talk affirmations written on sticky notes or inspirational conferences in the world can't guarantee that you'll always be happy, content, and satisfied.

No matter how wonderful your family or partner is or how much you love your job, there will still be times when you're just not functioning at your optimum level and you feel out of sorts. There's a little patch of gray hovering over your head, and you can't seem to get out from under it.

Maybe you're faced with illness, loss, change, or an emotion you can't put your finger on… but you know what? You can choose to be okay with not being okay. You can allow yourself this moment—whether it lasts an afternoon, a day, or a week—to not be completely in sync and to not have it all together.

Trying to force yourself back on top isn't always the quickest way to climb. Say out loud, "This, too, shall pass," and know that it will! Life is full of ebbs and flows, highs and lows. Learn to ride them out instead of fighting tooth and nail, exhausting yourself in the process. *Be okay with not being okay.*

Be
Inclusive

No one likes to be left out—to be the one who doesn't get invited, isn't greeted with a smile, or never gets to enter the conversation. We all want to belong. We want to feel like our opinions matter, our efforts count, and our values are shared by the people around us.

Including others will cost you, though. You don't get to stay snug and secure within the little circle of familiarity you've so carefully formed and where you feel protected. Instead you have to step outside that group to embrace those skirting cautiously around the edges, unsure where they fit in or belong. You might have to extend the circle of friends and coworkers you interact with and broaden the guest list for events you plan.

Inclusive embraces. It welcomes. It says, "Hey, there's room for you here." So scoot over a tad, make some space, and *be inclusive.*

Be in
the Flow

by Seb

Tesh and I went for a walk on the beach the other day. The tide was unusually low, exposing a field of rocks and pebbles. We continued along, jumping from rock to rock at a faster and faster pace. As we warmed up and got in tune with our bodies, we began skipping across those rocks faster than I thought would be possible without falling. Neither of us spoke—there was just a gleeful giggle from time to time.

With my attention focused entirely on where my feet would touch and push off next, there was no room for me to look at anything else. There was no fear of what would happen if I missed and no doubt that I could. There was just the mindfulness of flowing from rock to rock.

That's when it occurred to me that maybe this is the state of being that lets us achieve great things that lie beyond thinking and planning. This is not to say that planning and thinking ahead don't have their place. But no one has ever solved a problem, created a piece of art, built a house, or even completed a doctoral thesis solely through thinking.

While thought is the important first step of the creative process, once you have made up your mind and determined a course of action, further thinking may not be useful. In fact, the constant urge to think it through one more time—without taking action—may just be a form of procrastination. Only when you give your undivided attention to what you are doing can you get into this wonderfully flowing state that makes you forget time and brings joy to whatever you do.

To get into this state, thinking and planning need to be separated from implementing and executing. Don't consume information and try to create something at the same time. It may take a bit of practice, especially in our thought-consumed lives where we seldom have the space to concentrate without the distraction of new information coming into our consciousness. However, it's certainly worth practicing, not only because it boosts productivity but also because everything is more fun when you're flowing.

Try it out next time you have a problem to solve or challenge to overcome. Think carefully and choose your course of action before you start anything. Then give it all you've got. *Be in the flow.*

Be
Industrious

I love watching ants—they're always on the move. There's somewhere to be, food to find and bring back, and other ant friends to pass on important messages to. Same with bees—they are the captains of the honey industry, flying busily from flower to flower with purpose. I don't think there's ever been a day when a bee or an ant woke up and said, "Hmm, nothing to do today. Might as well just stay in bed."

Being industrious is invigorating. You're working with your hands and your mind, and you're using your talents and skills to contribute to or achieve a goal you've set. It's a careful balance, of course. Getting lots achieved without a clear purpose may be industrious, but it won't be fulfilling. Always being busy, with no time to rest and enjoy the present, won't be enriching either. But once you've found that priceless balance, you'll have discovered that being industrious isn't a drag; it's actually very satisfying.

If you wake up in the morning with purpose, look forward to jumping out of bed and into your latest project, and get up even earlier on the weekends purely because you're motivated by what the day has in store for you, then congratulations! Like the ants and the bees, you know how to *be industrious*.

Be
There

It seems that when bad things happen, there usually isn't much you can do. Be it your uncle's house getting damaged in an earthquake, a family friend passing away, or your child having a terrible experience at school… by the time you find out, it has already happened. You can't reverse, change, or make it go away with money, flowers, or well-intentioned platitudes. All you can really do is show up or be available for a phone call, a hug, and a listening ear.

When something bad happens to someone you care about, the speed with which you drop everything else to be there is all that matters. You might feel frustrated and it may even feel pointless. There could be other fires to put out that require your attention more urgently. But just remember… your love is needed. Your very presence is enough. Make the time to *be there*.

Be Interested

have two new friends—both very sweet young girls who don't pause for a breath between their rush of questions:

"Were you born in New Zealand?"
"Do you have a mum?"
"How about a dad?"
"What's your favorite color?"
"I like your hat—where did you buy it?"

When my conversation with these two girls ends, I've learned something (besides the vital information that they like their teachers, don't like their brothers, and both love pink): children are very good at being interested. They love to ask questions, hand out compliments like candy, and give you massive smiles in exchange for your attention. Everything about their body language says, "I like you. I'm interested in you. I want to be your friend."

I'm not sure at what age we start forgetting this amazing skill, but I think it's worth the effort to try to recapture it. We need to replace our texting with real-life interactions and our glazed-over eyes with smiles. We need to stop thinking about ourselves long enough to ask thoughtful questions of the people in front of us. If four-year-olds can do it, I bet we can too. Let's *be interested*.

Be Authentic

It's pretty easy to tell when a purchase isn't "the real deal." The taste is off, the quality is poor, or something about it just doesn't seem quite right.

We are willing to invest in an authentic pair of brand-name shoes rather than settle for their fake counterparts. We'll pay for the genuine article because we want the assurance of quality and satisfaction.

This is true not only of products but of people as well: we want to talk to and work with "real deal" people. We've all had experiences with time-wasters, liars, cheaters, hypocrites, and gossipmongers. The world needs people who actually do what they say they will do, keep their values intact no matter whom they're with, and offer a fully aligned, integrated "whole" self to friends, family, and coworkers alike.

Who wants to settle for an imitation that won't last? You'll find that people are more than willing to invest in you when you strive to *be authentic*.

Be
Decisive

Whether you're hoping to run a business, choosing what to study, or picking a new hobby, life requires decisions to be made at every turn. Many people prefer to procrastinate—to pull an ostrich maneuver and wedge their heads firmly in the sand until they're forced to come up for air. But you can spare yourself all the agonizing and hiding from reality by learning how to be decisive.

Here are three steps to make this easier:

- *Narrow down your options, and then pick one.* It doesn't have to be perfect (nothing is) or come with a sign from God; it just has to be a course of action.

- *Once you've made your choice, stick with it.* Don't berate yourself if it doesn't work out exactly how you planned. Don't tell yourself you could have done so much better. You *already* did better, because you were brave enough to give it a go.

- *Learn from your decisions.* Decisions come with consequences that could be perceived as good or bad, but really they're neither—they're just lessons. Take what you learned and apply that knowledge to your next decision.

This process will get easier the more you do it and the more in tune you become with yourself and your values. Trust your gut. While others are floundering in a sea of options, you'll be moving forward with purpose. *Be decisive.*

Be
Silent

A wise Indian guru Sri Sri Ravi Shankar wrote: "A question creates violence, wonder creates silence." I think about times of wonder. When we behold incredible art, amazing feats of courage, and landscapes that take our breath away, there is only one response that seems appropriate. We sink into silence. In the depths of silence our souls are free to express true emotion.

Words are only noise unless they give birth to silence. How much of what we say is even original, necessary, helpful, or life giving? Precious little, when you stop and think about it.

There's enough noise in this world already. Take some time today to push the mute button and… *be silent.*

Be
Content

I've got a lot of stuff. There are clothes in my closet, knickknacks on my dresser, and stray items clogging up my handbag that prevent me from locating my wallet in a hurry. I have the assurance of money coming into my bank account each week and working arms and legs that allow me to go wherever I desire. So why does this feeling come along every now and then that tells me I need more? It tells me that someone else might have what I want and deserve—that the writer elsewhere in cyberspace uses fancier words or the coworker across the meeting table is smarter, stronger, and more competent.

It's almost like life is designed to coax us toward discontent, so we're always striving and never reaching that elusive end goal of perfection. But who really wants to spend their precious hours on this planet wanting things they don't have while failing to enjoy what is right in front of them? Not me.

It takes a big person to create a mindset of plenty rather than want. Choosing to be content frees up space. Instead of holding on to things too tightly, let go and allow your hands to be open to receive. Make some room in your life. *Be content.*

Be
Ready

Life is happening all around you. People are making decisions, having great ideas, looking for partnerships, and wondering how they're going to get the ball rolling.

Are you ready?

If the opportunity of a lifetime came up and tried to shake your hand, would you smile and say hello or keep busily working away... waiting until five o'clock rolls around so you can head home?

Those who look for opportunities tend to find them. Don't get so attached to routine that you miss out on a chance to make something big happen. *Be ready.*

Be
Gritty

I watched a fascinating TED Talk given by teacher and psychologist Angela Lee Duckworth. She outlined what separates a successful student who is able to achieve from another who can't quite hit their potential.

Studies have proven it isn't IQ level, family income, home situation, race, or gender that make the difference… it all comes down to one little, not-often-mentioned quality: grit. Students with grit are determined to achieve, and so they do. Same with people in corporate jobs, pilots in training, and athletes… no matter what we set out to do, if we have a decent amount of grit, then we are more likely to reach our goals.

So what is grit? It's stickability or pressing on when the going gets tough and everyone else has gone. It's the determination to keep on track and to reach the outcome you want to achieve.

If you think about grit in a material sense, it's a roughness. It's got character. You can't wash it away and smooth it over without effort—it's tough and it isn't budging. Grit doesn't just show up in your life. You've got to build it in daily through proving to yourself that you *do* have the willpower to make things happen and stay true to your decisions.

Start with small things. Keep those little promises to yourself, and don't quit before the job is done. Eventually you'll become a person with grit. You'll increase your own chances of succeeding, no matter what it is you put your mind to. *Be gritty.*

Be
a Fighter

What are you fighting for? A parking space? First place at the checkout? A promotion? We have small battles every day that leave us more exhausted than triumphant. But perhaps we would find more satisfaction in our toils if we felt we were in the thick of something worth fighting for.

History's greatest warriors didn't carry guns, destroy smaller companies, or stomp on toes as they raced to the top of a corporate ladder.

For people like Mahatma Gandhi, Dr. Martin Luther King, Jr., Mother Teresa, Abraham Lincoln, Nelson Mandela, Florence Nightingale, and Rosa Parks—their weapons of choice were words, love, hope, inspiration, big ideas, leadership, and standing up when others were content to stay under the radar.

There are so many needs in our world... which one grabs your heart, inspires you to take action, and perhaps, even without the face-paint and armor, *be a fighter*?

Be a
Conscious Consumer

Let's take a step back and think about what it is that we're consuming. Where did it come from? How was it made? And, on a more spiritual note, what kind of energy went into making it?

An article of clothing produced in a sweatshop that you can purchase for five dollars may not be as much fun to wear as something carefully handmade from organic fabric or even rescued from a secondhand shop.

You may think it's silly to talk about clothes as if they can have an impact on your psyche, and in the past I probably would have agreed with you. But the more I investigate the world and talk to people who are making a conscious effort to know the origins of what they're eating, wearing, and using, the more I realize how interconnected everything is. It's like the butterfly effect theory: a small movement on one side of the world kicks off a chain of events that eventually reaches you in some way.

The processed food we purchase from supermarkets has often been stripped of a lot of its nutritional value. In the same way, clothing and household items may have been made at the expense of other people's livelihood, land, or cherished natural resources. We may not be directly causing these actions, but our purchases are still silent cogs in the supply chain.

Becoming a conscious consumer isn't easy. It requires a labyrinth of questions, research, and opinions to navigate in order to make educated, conscious buying decisions that you can feel good about.

Still… any effort you can make, even if it's simply the decision to only buy fair-trade chocolate or ethically produced jewelry, is a step in the right direction. You'll start your own butterfly effect, one little action at a time, when you choose to *be a conscious consumer.*

Be
Open

I like watching people meet each other for the first time. In the moment after the introduction, there's always a "sizing up" that takes place. You can see it as each person examines the other, wondering how much they have in common, what the other person thinks of them, and how much or how little to share of themselves.

We tend to feel our chances of making friends or getting along with others will increase if we have something in common with them and are able to fit in. Perhaps this feeling goes right back to the playground: not wanting to be that lonely kid by ourselves on the swings. But over the last few years I've been changing my approach a little. Rather than trying to pull a chameleon and be what I hope the person in front of me is expecting or comfortable with, I choose to just be open. I find the open-book approach refreshing and effective. As I share of myself, others feel that they have permission to open up too.

Most of the time, we err too much on the side of secrecy, pointless small talk, facades, and a closed-off attitude that says, "You give first, and I'll possibly consider handing back a morsel of information in exchange."

Openness wins friends, clients, business partners, and opportunities; most of all, it inspires confidence and authenticity because you're not hiding anything.

So next time you're doing that awkward, we've-just-met dance, why not try to *be open*.

Be
Equanimous
by Seb

I once thought that in order to live a life of happiness I needed to do what felt good and avoid what didn't.

After chasing the sensual pleasure of riding perfect waves and avoiding anything that didn't feel like fun, I eventually came to realize otherwise.

When we are merely pursuing pleasant emotions and sensations, we quickly find ourselves torn between things we either want or hope to avoid. We want to become successful but avoid failing; we want pleasure but no pain; we want inner peace and harmony but become annoyed when our inner peace is interrupted.

Shifting between grasping and avoidance creates an unstable foundation for building lasting happiness. Instead we can develop an unshakable evenness of mind, an inner equipoise that cannot be upset by the emotions or sensations we experience. We can enable our minds to do what we know is right regardless of how we feel so that our minds will be truly free.

Next time you find your actions being affected by how or what you feel, decide to regain your freedom and do what is right regardless. Decide to *be equanimous.*

Be
Alone

If you're a people person, an extrovert, or generally outgoing, you might find this idea a little odd at first. Being alone? Who wants to be alone?

I'm not recommending the hermit lifestyle or withdrawing from the world in an isolated effort to "find" yourself. It seems that some people don't have the capacity to be alone—to enjoy their own company, to not require the constant stimulus, chatter, and affirmation that comes from having other people always around or close by.

One friend told me that she can't handle being by herself. It makes her nervous, uncomfortable, and paranoid. Perhaps you identify with this. Maybe you find yourself always seeking out others and need "moral support" to attend an event.

Have you ever stopped to question this urge? Society often ridicules "loners" and promotes being part of a group. But it shows a sense of strength and self-appreciation when you can spend a contented evening in just your own company—when you can go on a walk without needing a buddy to go with you or a smartphone to fill your ears with noise, or when you want to do something and no one can come along, you can say, "No worries—I'll just go by myself."

If being alone terrifies you, take a look inside and find out why that is. Your best chances to reflect, grow, tune in, and have moments of inspiration will often only come when you're alone—not distracted or engaged with other people. Just you. It might take a while to adjust, but there are times when it's quietly satisfying to simply *be alone*.

Be an Energy-Giver

by Seb

There is a certain kind of person whose company makes me feel more alive and somehow more energized. I've been thinking about what it is these people do and don't do so I can better understand what makes a great energy-giver:

- They smile at everyone with genuine warmth that shows their love for their fellow human beings.

- They enthusiastically look for opportunities to serve others, generally doing more than required. (They are the ones who stay after your dinner party and happily do the dishes without making you feel guilty.)

- They look for the good, talk about happy news, and deflect any gossip or negativity.

- They are sparing with their criticism and lavish in their praise.

- They generally have a great sense of humor and laugh easily, and they make you feel good because of it.

- They tend to be generous with their resources and spend very little on themselves.

They are always trying new things and passionately sharing what they've recently learned, motivating others to do the same.

They don't presume or take for granted or have expectations or get disappointed. They are generally grateful and openly express their thanks for whatever life offers them.

The energy-giver expends as much energy as possible, mostly for others. As a result, he or she seems to be more energetic, joyful, and happy. It's nothing new, really—it's the old principle of "the more you give, the more you get" applied to everyday life. It works in all situations, everyone can do it, and it costs you nothing but some life energy, which you'll get back in droves.

If we all give a little more energy and enthusiasm to what we do, we'll create a brighter, more energetic world. *Be an energy-giver.*

Be
Active

Getting your body moving is one of the best things you can do for your long-term health, your energy levels, and your self-confidence. We live in a sit-down society where we work all day at a desk, then spend an hour seated driving home—only to plant ourselves in front of the television for the evening.

While we all know it's important to be active, it's something that often takes a low spot on our priority list. So here are five quick tips for keeping your blood pumping and your brain clear:

1. *Stretch.* Spend ten to fifteen minutes first thing in the morning doing some stretches. Swing your arms around, do a couple of lunges, or reach up high and then bend down to touch your toes. It doesn't have to be a fancy routine; just working out the kinks from sleeping will get you off to a good start.

2. *Take the farthest parking space.* Instead of spending twenty minutes circling around and around hoping to find the closest parking spot, park far away. Think of the brisk walk as a mini-workout.

3. *Join a class.* There is much to be said for group motivation. Committing to a class and paying for it makes it much more likely you'll show up than if you promise yourself you'll go for a run three times a week. Try a hip-hop or spin class, kickboxing, Zumba, fencing, or karate. If it's something you've never done before, even better!

4. *Love stairs.* Elevators are a useful but lazy invention. The next time you've got a meeting on the fourth floor, take the stairs. Treat each step as a helpful fitness friend.

5. *Dance!* Put on music while you're cooking dinner and bust out a few moves in between stirring. If you work from home, take a few minutes every couple of hours to groove to the radio. Skip while you walk, spin while you wait, or step while you watch the news. It's fun, it gets your heart rate up, and it's 100 percent free.

People often put themselves in a "not sporty" box: "Me? Join your pickup basketball game? Oh, no! I'm too uncoordinated!" Don't put limits on yourself. You don't have to be a quarterback to lead an active life. Just try incorporating some of these little energy boosters into your day and see how much better you feel. *Be active.*

Be
Focused

Do you find yourself switching from one thing to another a lot? Are you jumping from your e-mail inbox to your Facebook feed; surfing TV channels; frantically clicking your mouse; texting while driving; eating while getting dressed for work; going for a walk while making phone calls? Do you feel like there's always something else you should be checking on or doing, even while you're trying to get one thing ticked off your to-do list?

I often feel like this, and when I'm in this headspace, nothing seems to get done. The first step to conquering any bad habit (and a fidgety, fluttery, short attention-span *is* a habit) is awareness. Once you become aware, you can start to do something about it.

When you only focus on one thing at a time, it's amazing how proficient you can be. Look at star athletes, professional opera singers, master chefs—they're not off trying to be clowns, orchestra conductors, or pilots at the same time! Their careers are focused. And it's that focus that makes them successful.

Next time you catch yourself trying to do three things at once, pause, take a deep breath, and remind yourself to focus. Your productivity will increase and your enjoyment of each task will be much greater. *Be focused.*

Be
Unrealistic

Remember when you were younger and you enthusiastically told someone your big dream? They looked at you with a knowing smile (the one that says, "I love you and I don't want you to get hurt") and offered up a gentle warning: "That sounds wonderful—just remember to be realistic."

But what really audacious, world-changing goal ever sounded realistic from the outset? Realistic means it's real *now*—you can see it, measure it, predict it, and control it. Why can't we be *un*realistic, challenging the parameters of what we've always been told is possible by making new discoveries, pushing boundaries, and daring to think bigger and in newer directions than those who came before us?

We've had "be realistic" drilled into us for too long. It's time to embrace our childlike sense of wonder again, bring back our big ideas and plans, and for a refreshing change *be unrealistic.*

Be
a Reader

Growing up in a small town, more than anything I wanted to get out and go places... so I read.

I read all the books in the children's section in our small library. Then the young adult books. Then I moved to the adult section for more material. I borrowed my parents' books on business, relationships, and personal development. I read all the works of Shakespeare, Jane Austen, Louisa May Alcott, John Maxwell, Ted Dekker, Stephen Covey, Robert Jordan, Stephen Lawhead, Robin Hobb, and Willard Price. I read books about animals, magic, leadership, tradition, and foreign countries... books that opened up new worlds of possibility and new ways of thinking.

Reading is a learner's golden egg. With a book or online written material, you can find out just about anything you want to know.

I've met people who say they hate reading. When I ask them why, the usual answer is that as children they were forced to read things they had absolutely no interest in. They associate pain and frustration with reading. The wonderful thing about being an adult is that now you're free to choose! It's never too late to develop an appreciation for all the research, communication, and personal development possibilities that reading brings.

Here are three tips for becoming a reader:

1. *Read what interests you.* Follow your passions, and reading will become effortless. Don't struggle through a book just because someone said you "had" to read it. Just like anything in life, it's more fun to read out of enjoyment than obligation.

2. *Read in small chunks.* We're all busy people, and sometimes reading a whole book can seem like an impossible mission. Try committing to one chapter a day or even just a couple of pages. Eventually you'll finish and feel great about it.

3. *Use content compilation apps.* If you're mainly an online reader, these apps allow you to create a "magazine" around your own interests.

This is certainly one habit in life that's worth developing. *Be a reader.*

Be
Tidy

Mess can be distracting. I personally find it hard to concentrate when I'm surrounded by clutter—my thoughts get lost in the jumble, and finding clarity becomes a game of hide-and-seek.

Mess doesn't happen all at once, though. It gradually builds. It's sneaky and persistent, but easy to combat if you're committed to a few simple "tidy" principles:

- *Put things away.* Sounds kind of obvious, right? But when you're in a rush, it takes effort to not just leave the scissors on the table, your clothes on the floor, and a wet towel hastily thrown over a chair as you run off to the next thing. If you use something, put it back where you found it.

- *Clean as you go.* Whenever I cook, my goal is to finish with as few dirty dishes as possible. I'll clean a pan while something else is heating or wash the dishes as the food is cooking in the oven. It's very satisfying to finish making a meal and not have much work to do afterward. This approach applies to everything: wipe a counter, dust when you see something that needs it, or clean the mark on the carpet when you spot it (not a week later).

Not using it? Time to say goodbye! I don't want to reach seventy and have a house full of presents I didn't use, mugs at the back of the cupboard no one reaches for, clothes with tags still on them, or boxes of useless knickknacks that my relatives will have to clean out when I'm gone. Most of the time, if we don't need it now, it's unlikely we'll need it later (or even be able to find it if we do!). Have a garage sale, donate to a charity, or give your unused items to a friend who will actually use them. It's easier to be tidy when you have fewer things to find places for.

Your environment reflects how you think and how you work. As it becomes more efficient and open, so will you.

Pay attention to the space around you, treat the things you do need with care, and let go of the things you don't. Soon you'll find it's easy to *be tidy*.

Be an Early Riser

Successful people seem to have something in common, and it's not educated parents, attractive features, or a natural knack for numbers. It's actually a pretty simple habit, which when repeated can have a powerful impact: they get an early start to the day.

Successful people recognize the value of having a head start. They use that extra hour or two to accomplish a task or spend time exercising, meditating, or brainstorming. They feed their souls before getting swept away in the oncoming wave of schedules, meetings, and demands, like dogs that need walking, kids that need feeding, and e-mails that need reading.

The early morning is yours. It's fresh, untainted, and waiting for you. For me, the key to getting up early is making it past the "push-through" moment. You know the one—it's when you've partially sat up and you're starting to toss the warmth of your covers away and brush off your clinging dreams. But then the pull of your soft pillow draws your head back down for "just another ten minutes." My ten minutes usually turn into another hour or so, leaving me feeling like I'm already running behind by the time I get up.

But if you can make it past the push-through moment, you'll be rewarded by a blank canvas early morning of crisp air, clear thought, and the satisfying feeling of being able to focus on what you *want* to get done, not just on what *needs* to be done.

Even if it's hard at first, you can *be an early riser.*

Be Silly

Sometimes I wonder how we all ended up so serious— working "real" jobs, always aware of how we look and presenting the "right" image; making polite conversation over cheese and wine at social events; going to committee meetings; following the rules; and trying to impress others with our intelligence and social skills.

When do we ever allow ourselves to just be silly? To do stuff just because it's fun, not because it's important? To giggle and laugh uncontrollably until we collapse and our tummies hurt... to say the thoughts that pop into our heads without overanalyzing them for suitability before sharing... to chase, skip, jump, and dance with abandon without caring about who's watching or what they're thinking?

It's so freeing when you allow yourself to be silly. Your muscles relax, your smile grows wider, and you experience that joy you used to feel as a child at play. And instead of judging you, the people around you might even thank you for awakening that long-lost feeling in them!

Our workplaces, homes, and friendships could all benefit from a little more silliness. Silliness gives us the power to laugh at ourselves, to realize that life really isn't such a big, difficult struggle, and to see that the little things we find annoying can actually be quite funny.

So stop overthinking. Give yourself some freedom to chill out, live spontaneously, and *be silly*.

Be
Detached

Buddhism is built on the principle of detachment, and I've discovered that it's a central belief to many other religions as well. But it's certainly not a core ideal of secular society. In direct contrast to the "must have more" attitude of materialism, it dares to tell us that, in fact, we need *less* and what we already have shouldn't define us.

Our relationships, our possessions, our careers, and the things that happen to us on a day-to-day basis should be treated as separate from us, not essential to our ability to function, love, or feel joy. By practicing detachment, we free ourselves from expectations, which can lead to disappointments, misunderstandings, and pain.

For example, say I have my heart set on being taken to a favorite restaurant for my birthday. I've been telling myself it's the one thing I really want to make my day special, and I'm already visualizing the delicious dinner I'm going to have. We drive there only to find that it's closed for renovations. I could allow this to ruin my whole birthday. I could complain, perhaps even cry. I could choose to be dissatisfied with any alternate dinner option suggested. Or, if I practiced the art of detachment, I could be open to the possibility of discovering a new favorite restaurant or going for an outdoor picnic instead and having a wonderful birthday dinner regardless. The circumstance doesn't need to determine my level of happiness.

I used to sail to the highest heights and then come crashing down again just as fast if things didn't go exactly how I'd planned. By being 100 percent attached to my anticipated outcomes, I pinned everything on my expectations rather than on reality. One very even-keeled friend pointed out that if I could keep my expectations in check, I'd be able to achieve a steadier, more balanced life. At first I scoffed and told him this sounded pretty boring. Now years down the track, having explored more religions, I see even more the wisdom of the practice of detachment. It's beautiful in simplicity and can be applied to nearly every situation.

The next time you hear yourself saying, "It would be so awful if _____ didn't work out," replace that emotion with detachment. You may find that things have a way of working out for the best when instead of making your happiness dependent on a particular outcome, you choose to *be detached*.

Be Selective

There was a time when I said *yes* to just about anything—new friends, new opportunities, new clients, new places, new events, new causes to give money to or volunteer for. It was fun. I learned a lot, experienced things I wouldn't have otherwise, and ended up with heaps of people in my circle and plenty of work to do. But eventually, it all became a bit too much.

Racing to a different social event every night; trying to remember all the birthdays, babies, and things going on in your friends' lives; working late to make sure your clients are happy—this is a recipe for exhaustion.

So I've become more selective. I don't make instant best friends with everyone I have a conversation with. I choose the events I go to carefully by asking myself if they will fulfill something in my life or support something I truly believe in. I have reached a place where I'm not afraid to say goodbye to a client who drains too much energy from me or who isn't in line with my values. I try to find ways to give back to my community that will have the most impact.

Being selective has brought me more calm, more enjoyment, and a deeper connection to who I really am and what I really want to do.

Take the time to think about your choices of friends, entertainment, clients, events, and causes—*be selective.*

Be
Personal

Today, more than ever, being personal matters. Find ways to show others that you're human, that you realize they're human, and that you care. The holidays are a fantastic time to practice this. Instead of buying something for your family members, make them gifts that will mean something to them. Put love into each detail; use recycled paper with handwritten messages written on it to wrap them in.

Say *no* to the standard bottle of wine and box of chocolates for your clients. Write personal holiday cards to each one. Surely there's more you can say than just "Hope you have a happy holiday!"

One year we made candles in recycled jars and teacups. Another year we made soaps with fresh lavender cut from our garden and sand collected at the beach. Each one had a plantable gift tag embedded with seeds that grew either delicious basil or fragrant wildflowers.

Yes, it took time.
Yes, it took effort.
But was it worth it?
YES!

Add a little more humanness to the world, and choose to *be personal*.

Be
Concise

If you can say it in less words, do. If you can make a point without needing to slip in three subpoints, make it. If you can cut your e-mails in half by turning your paragraphs into bullet points and idle conversation into something others can understand instantly without getting a headache, then please do this.

It's being concise.

There's too much going on already—too many words clogging our inboxes and demanding our brain space. If you know how to be concise, you've also mastered how to be understood. And amongst all the chatter, this is valuable.

Don't overthink it. Don't overwrite it. *Be concise.*

Be
Relaxed

There's a funny rule with the universe: if you're stressed, things go wrong; if you're relaxed, things seem to just flow. I took the relaxed route on a recent overseas trip. Even when it seemed that I'd miss a flight, the shuttle was going too slow, or I was at the wrong train platform, the second I felt my heart rate going up and my brain rushing to pump out a million different scenarios of what could go wrong, I made the decision to be relaxed. I told myself that everything was fine and everything would work out. And you know what? It did.

Somehow, I got where I needed to go when I needed to get there and I found the thing, place, or person I was looking for—all without raising my blood pressure and adding worry lines to my forehead!

Often, the things we stress about are completely out of our control. They're not worth the time spent producing the negative energy.

When I am stressed, I lose my ability to think clearly. I fumble, I drop things, and I say stupid things. Maybe you've experienced a similar stress-induced fog. Simply by making the choice to relax, I can free up my brain space to operate more efficiently.

A relaxed approach to life doesn't make you lazy and it doesn't make you less productive. It actually makes you nicer to be around and allows you to expand your awareness to the needs of the people surrounding you.

So in the words of a relaxation expert: don't worry, be happy. *Be relaxed.*

Be
Abundant

by Seb

Like most First World country dwellers, I am able to afford anything I need to live a basic happy and healthy life. Despite having all I need, I used to feel a desire to preserve what I had and to be more thrifty and careful with my giving to others and to myself.

Even though I knew my bank account would shrink when I decided to leave my corporate job to follow my passion, a feeling of unease and concern crept over me the third month it happened in a row. However, I am not convinced that a tight grip on my money and more thrifty and resource-constrained behavior would have made me feel better.

When you confirm to the world around you that you need something, it just creates vibes of scarcity and interrupts the flow of resources and wealth to you. So instead of worrying about your savings account, ask yourself if your spending aligns with your principles and if it will increase your abundance in the long-term. Does it serve you?

Buying lunch for a friend? Yep, it is an investment in a relationship. Grabbing takeout for lunch just because it's convenient? Nope, doesn't serve you. Buying organic, healthy, but pricey groceries? Absolutely, this gives you more energy and preserves your long-term health—go nuts! Ordering yet another fancy pair of dress shoes? That's not an investment in abundance. Buying your friend a thank-you present because he hooked you up with a new client or business connection? That's a must. Investing in programs or life coaching that will make you a better, fitter, more knowledgeable, more effective person? Go for it!

These are just a few examples, but I think you get the idea. When you expend your resources on something, don't worry too much about the dent in your bank account; instead, be aware of the long-term benefits it brings to you. If there are none, consider not buying it.

Abundance comes from not worrying about your resources, knowing that you have everything you need and that your supply is limitless. However, you can only truly feel abundant if you don't waste your resources, but invest them with purpose in other people and things that serve you. When you do this consistently, you might be surprised how effortlessly plenty of what you need flows your way. *Be abundant.*

Be
Second

Anyone who has ever played a game with me knows how much I love to win. I will fight to the very end, form alliances, beg for rematches, and let out a victory cry for every point scored. Like a lot of people, I love the feeling of winning.

But lately I've been noticing and admiring the people who are happy to be second—those behind-the-scenes people who get stuff done, stick around to clean up after the big event, and wear the same smile whether the points are going their way or not. They're the people who sacrifice their own goals and dreams to support something bigger and make sure it happens. They're satisfied to live life honorably rather than gloriously.

Being okay with being second can cause conflicting emotions. Why be the person pushing someone else up over the last lip of the mountain instead of driving in the stake yourself? Yet, where has the me-first, I-win-you-lose approach to life gotten us so far? Nowhere beautiful.

Any thriving, loving community needs people who are okay with staying out of the limelight—people who truly put others first so that they can, for the good of us all… *be second*.

Be
Smiley

Happiness and positive energy seem to be directly linked with this facial expression. It's pretty hard to be grumpy when you're smiling. Smiling releases endorphins, makes you look more attractive to others, and generally lifts the mood wherever you are.

There's a lot to love about smiling. It costs nothing, it's easy to do, and in only two seconds you can cheer up the person in front of you.

One of the best moments you can have with a stranger is a shared smile. Suddenly, without ever saying a word, you're united through a universal expression of friendship, peace, connectedness, and joy.

If we could all make it a habit to smile more, it would be a happier world. *Be smiley.*

Be Trusting

People today tend to err on the side of caution with nearly everything—new people, new places, new products. You're advised to be careful, be wary, have your wits about you, don't get taken advantage of, make sure you stand your ground, go out at night in pairs, stash things away, keep an eye out at all times... I'm sure you've been on the receiving end of some of these warnings before.

And while I'm not saying there isn't some wisdom in these, I do think that a world full of fear isn't a great place to be. Distrust breeds distrust. If I treat you like you're going to cheat me, perhaps you will. After all, then you'll just be meeting my expectations.

Before leaving on a trip to Bangkok, I would have had to use all my fingers and toes to count the cautions I received: don't talk to anyone, look out for scammers, stay inside at night, and don't trust the taxi drivers. When I arrived, at first I was hesitant to even smile at people in case they used that as a sign to target me! But soon I decided that I didn't want to travel that way.

I'd prefer to operate on the basic premise that people are good and if you give them the chance, they'll prove themselves trustworthy. And in just the first few days of my trip I received help from complete strangers, was given hand-drawn maps and directions when I was lost, got advice on places to go, had people help me across busy streets and offer me food to try for free, and got lots of returned smiles! Is it still possible to get cheated by being trusting? Yes. Could people potentially take advantage of you? Yes.

But ask yourself: What's the alternative? A life of fearful, sideways looks at those around you? Never saying *yes* to opportunities for fear something might go wrong or it won't turn out to be quite as good as you thought? Better to expect the best than to always be prepared for the worst. You might be amazed at how people value and respect your trust when you give it freely.

Trust your gut, believe that good things will happen, and *be trusting.*

Be
Hospitable

There's something lovely about being hosted—being welcomed, eating delicious food carefully prepared for you, participating in warm conversation and laughter, and not even having to do the dishes afterward!

Good hosts make you feel at ease. They share. They show how much they care by including you in conversation, asking thoughtful questions, and accommodating your food and beverage preferences. They put in an effort to make you feel like part of their family. And it's a pretty amazing feeling to find a home away from your own.

Do you enjoy being hospitable? Are you the person who bends over backward to put everyone at ease, making sure each guest who enters your home feels like they are welcome and appreciated? It may not be your natural inclination. Perhaps it seems like too much effort and you're happy to leave it to your other half or parent or roommates to take on the role of host. But next time you're having people over, try it on for size.

A little hospitality can go a long way. Maybe someone in your circle needs a place to stay for a night or two, a friend has just moved into the area and doesn't know many people, or an older relative has lost their partner and floats around the house each day, lonely.

Keep on the lookout for ways to *be hospitable*.

Be an
Experience Creator

One night we had friends over for dinner. On the menu was Thai fish curry. Instead of setting the table with forks, spoons, and knives, Seb suggested we use some mussel shells he'd found on the beach. We told our guests we were eating "traditional Thai" style tonight, and it was shells-only cutlery! They loved it. And when they talk about that dinner, what they'll remember won't be the food but how we ate it—a new experience.

Another time, I told Seb we were heading to a café for lunch, but once we hopped in the car I gave him a riddle to solve. This ended up leading us, via a series of increasingly tricky clues, to a surprise night away in an off-the-grid earth house. I could have just told him I'd booked us a night away, but I wanted to create an experience he'd remember.

The act of experience-creating brings fun, romance, and sparkle into situations. It takes some imagination, some planning, and a sense of childlike playfulness to really get into creating experiences for people, but once you start, you'll be hooked. Presents become more inventive; dinner parties become themed, dress-up, or uniquely located; and holidays develop an element of surprise!

Think about what sort of experiences you'd like to create for the people you love. Have some fun. Give new things a try. *Be an experience creator.*

Be
Self-Aware

People often ask me if I have any tips for managing a busy life. Although I could tell you to be a superstar with time management, color-code your to-do lists, and sync your online calendar with your phone, I actually think the best possible way to manage a busy life is by practicing being self-aware.

We all have natural ebbs and flows. Being aware of those and living within the boundaries they impose is what makes the difference between feeling stressed and feeling fulfilled.

Here are a few quick questions to help you determine your personal level of self-awareness:

1. Do you reflect back on events after they've occurred, assessing your responses in different situations? You might do this by asking yourself questions such as, "How did this person/that comment/those jokes make me feel?"

2. Can you sense your own moods, and do you have the control to consciously turn them around when you need to?

3. Are you able to predict your own response to a given set of stimuli? For instance, if you know in advance that attending a party where there will be lots of people is going to make you feel nervous and intimidated, do you know what to do to change that response?

If you're answering *yes* to these questions, then congratulations—you're self-aware already. But most of us rarely take the time to reflect back on our responses to situations and really analyze them to find the source of our behavior. It's even harder to actually change the way we know we'll usually respond to something.

While it may be difficult, it's only by being self-aware that we can ride the wave of life rather than be sucked down into every riptide that comes along. There's a saying I love: *If you always do what you've always done, you'll always get what you've always gotten.*

Your moods will change, guaranteed. Each month you'll have highs and lows, but if you know when they're coming, you can work with them, not against them. Think of getting to know yourself as a project. Step outside of the situation you're in and be your own observer.

"Know thyself" wasn't in the Socratic rule book for nothing. *Be self-aware.*

Be
Wild

Our roots are wild. We're descended from explorers, trailblazers, hunters and foragers, pioneers, and people who worked the land, faced down challenges, and never heard of insurance.

It's easy to forget that when you're sitting in an air-conditioned office on a padded chair with only mental stimulus and your ready-made supermarket dinner is waiting in the fridge at home.

Society wants to keep us tame, manageable, and easy to predict. But something in us cries out to be wild—to be out in nature, to get muddy and not care, to feel our blood really pumping, to yell and shout and just let go.

Being wild could be dancing in the rain, running as fast as you can on the beach or through the park, saying what you actually think instead of what's politically correct, breaking the rules occasionally… getting in touch with your primitive, intuitive self.

Embrace the raw, instinct-driven side within. Listen to those gut urges and what nature is telling you. Get out of the office, leave the comfort of home occasionally, and *be wild*.

Be
Worthy

Sometimes it can be hard to feel like you measure up. There always seems to be someone else who is better looking, more accomplished, more successful, or who has a more "together" home life, a nicer house, better-behaved children, wider networks, cooler clothing, or talents that you don't possess but secretly wish you did.

We're told we have to earn things by being a certain way. We have to put in the hard work, make the effort, dress right, wear the right labels, go to the right events, talk to the right people… no wonder it's difficult sometimes to accept good things when they come along!

We awkwardly brush off compliments, say *no* to the attractive person asking us out, hide in the back, and fear speaking up. We don't step forward to claim our spot in the limelight, take that promotion, or go after our dream—all because deep down inside there is this feeling that we're not worthy. We're not meant to be here. We're just faking it, and someday someone is going to call us out.

Well, you know what? You *are* here. You're a living, breathing soul inside a body, and if that were all you had to your name, it would be enough. Allow yourself to really become aware of the life surging through you. This is your gift, your status. You're a miracle—a little divine spark in earth's fireworks show—and if that wasn't true, you wouldn't be reading this right now.

You have a place, you have a purpose, and you are intrinsically, undeniably, unequivocally worthy. Don't cheat yourself by thinking otherwise. Accept it. Believe it. *Be worthy.*

Be Instinctive

by Seb

In an age where we seek certainty through research, measurement, and analysis, instinct sounds like something that belongs to a previous time. It is too primordial, too difficult to define. Besides, there are no university courses that teach it. To be instinctive in a sophisticated world is considered bad.

Instinct is a gift of nature formed through countless decades of evolutionary carving. It's that gut feeling that tells you whether that business deal is going to work before you've analyzed the numbers. It's that inner voice that tells you whether an idea is worth pursuing before you've done hours of research. It's that initial feeling you get way before a thought can evolve. It makes you know without knowing why.

Sadly, in a society that honors the rational mind, fewer and fewer people pay any attention to what their instincts are telling them. We are supposed to reason why we know something. If we can't articulate the "why," we risk being disbelieved and ridiculed. Yet when we are facing a big decision and desperate for guidance, our instinct is the most precious gift on earth.

So next time you get that gut feeling deep inside you, accept that you know and let the "why" mature over time. *Be instinctive.*

Be an
Initiator

I sometimes catch myself waiting. Waiting for someone else to come up with an idea. Waiting for a friend to let me know they've been thinking about me. Waiting for my partner to be the first to say "I'm sorry." Waiting for a situation to change so I'm happier, more content, or better off.

But nothing much tends to happen when you're passively waiting around for it. Chances are, everyone else is doing the same thing.

Being the initiator means you choose to step up and take responsibility for making your desired reality happen. It's getting your brain in gear to generate an awesome idea or plan that you can suggest to others. It's e-mailing your friend to say, "Hey, I appreciate you, I've been thinking about you, and I'd love to catch up soon—let's organize a time." It's swallowing your pride and being the first to say you're sorry. It's looking at an undesirable situation, figuring out the steps you need to take to improve it, and then taking them—immediately!

People love hanging out with an initiator. And by living life actively rather than passively, you empower others to live that way as well. Stop waiting, and *be an initiator.*

Be a
Problem Solver

There's a rare breed of people out there you don't often meet. They don't hang out with the glass-is-always-half-empty people who seem to be loudly present wherever you go. They're doing something else somewhere else—and you can bet it's a whole lot more fun. *They are the problem solvers.*

These people are more interested in fixing what's wrong than simply complaining about it to all their friends. Instead of stomping their feet and saying, "This service/product/person isn't doing what I want," they're busy asking questions: "What is the underlying problem here? How can I fill this gap? Who can help me?"

Problem solvers have a revolutionary perspective on problems. In fact, they don't even think of them as problems. They're dealing with challenges, temporary hiccups, learning curves, small obstacles on the certain route to success. They always find a way. You know why? Because they are *sure* it's there.

If you've been hanging out with the glass-is-always-half-empty people for too long, it's time to find a new crowd. *Be a problem solver.*

Be
Calm

had my first Buddhist meditation experience recently. In between the instructions to "clear your mind" and "let go of all tension" was one priceless little phrase that left the room with me that evening. After several slow, focused breaths, we were urged to take time to "abide in the calm."

"Abide" is such a deeply rooted sounding word. It isn't transient, coming and going like cars across a busy highway. It *dwells*.

Imagine being able to actually live in a state of calm— imperturbable, unfazed, and so grounded in your own sense of self that calmness permanently resides within you. It's very appealing and very possible.

Finding calm is a direct result of our response to any given circumstance. We can respond to our experiences with serenity or with panic, fear, and fluster. The latter options might be easier to choose but are infinitely more wearying. So next time you're affronted by an unexpected situation, pause and remember to take a moment to abide and *be calm*.

Be a
Treasure Hunter

Remember birthday party games like pin the tail on the donkey, hot potato, and musical chairs? My favorite was treasure hunt. We'd follow the clues (and in some cases, if Mom had enough time, an actual map!), decode the cryptic puzzles, and eventually, triumphantly find the goodie bag with a big "X" on top of it stashed away in some secret hiding place. Eating the treasure (usually chocolate coins) wasn't nearly half as much fun as finding it.

A friend recently told me how hard it was for him to engage with certain people at his work. "They just aren't very interesting to me. I don't see what we have in common, and they're so closed off that it's hard to build any bridges."

"Think of it as a treasure hunt!" I suggested. Work on the basis that every single person you meet will have a hidden gem—some interesting nugget that will surprise you, delight you, or teach you something. You just sometimes have to do a bit of digging to locate it.

Everyone has different facets and layers to themselves. I've met old people with amazing stories, young people with engaging wisdom, and people from all walks of life with fascinating hobbies, clever ideas, and unexpected pasts… it's all there, under the surface.

Once you decode the clues, follow the map, and ask the right questions, you'll get to the treasure. Try it with the next person you meet. *Be a treasure hunter.*

Be
Sparkly

Have you ever met someone who is so alive and full of energy that they almost glow? Their eyes light up when they smile, their voice is full of genuine warmth when they speak, and their body is infused with enthusiasm with every movement.

This is the kind of person who sparkles. You always come away from spending time with them feeling a little sparklier yourself—like you've just been sprinkled with some of Tinkerbell's pixie dust.

I don't think the world has enough sparkly people. Perhaps there's no specific recipe for it, but here's an acronym for guidance along the road to sparkliness:

Smile
Positively
And
Reach toward a
Kind,
Loving
You.

Be sparkly.

Be
Versatile

I love wearing hats: denim ones, leather ones, beanies, floppy hats, trilby hats, fancy hats, knitted hats. I like how when I put on a different hat, I feel I have a slightly different persona.

I apply that same theory to other areas of my life. When I approach a new challenge or task I wouldn't ordinarily do, I picture myself as wearing a different hat that day.

I put on my Tesh-the-Plumber hat when the shower gets clogged, my Tesh-Who-Figures-Out-Annoying-Technical-Problems hat when my computer isn't working, my Tesh-the-Accountant-Who-Can-Reconcile-Things-Accurately hat around tax time, and my Tesh-the-Resourceful-Inventor hat for times when I don't have a lot to work with!

It makes the task easier if I think of myself as someone in a new role, playing a part that perhaps doesn't feel intrinsically "me" but that I'm totally capable of doing. It makes it fun, and it makes me versatile. I'm not stuck doing the things I already know how to do—I'm empowered to approach something in a new way.

The next time you're confronted with a situation where you need to make a chameleon shift in order to get things done, remember how fun and easy it can be to just put on a new hat and *be versatile.*

Be
Creative

When's the last time you made something just for the fun of it? Not something you *had* to make, like dinner for your family or a project for work. Not something practical, profitable, or peer approved, but something simply beautiful, expressive, and creative.

It could be scrapbooking, card making, painting, sculpting, sketching clouds on a drawing pad, jewelry making, knitting, making a video, decorating a cake, writing a song, or designing a poster. Whatever form it takes, you will feel the thrill that comes from unleashing your inner creativity on a project and losing track of time while poring over your personal work of art.

In our serious, grownup lives, it can take real effort to be creative. Finger painting is no longer a regular afternoon activity. We're offered ready-made entertainment at every turn, so perhaps it's not surprising that in our spare time we're more likely to sit in front of a screen than to create beauty. But despite the mouthfuls of popcorn, our creative souls remain hungry. Consider creating some space in your life to *make* things. You could even find friends to collaborate with.

Relax, get inspired, and *be creative.*

Be a
Learner

Learning is the primary step toward anything worth doing. Do you want to be a great cook? You'll have to learn some recipes. Are you looking to succeed financially? You might need to spend some time learning investment principles.

Sometimes it seems as if learning is a chore. It conjures up images of grumpy schoolteachers, hard tests, and painful failures. And that perspective is exactly why many people are happy to stick with the skill set they already have, to keep doing the hobbies they've always done, and to stay in the same job they've been at for years. I'll let you in on a secret though… learning isn't a hardship. It's a joy.

Think about everything you love doing: singing, swimming, reading, making beautiful things, writing, or playing sports or an instrument. Were you born knowing how to do those things? Of course not!

Learning is growing. Learning is being able to share. It is gaining understanding, knowledge, wisdom, culture, and valuable perspective. If you decide to be a learner, you're set for life, because everything is interesting and each person you meet can be your teacher. Eventually, you'll be the one teaching others.

You really *can* learn something new every day. Surprise yourself. *Be a learner.*

Be Courageous

Courage is hard to write about. It can't be described so much as experienced. It comes when least expected but most needed. Courage fills you with the awareness that life—in all its many forms—is worth fighting for.

I've heard people use "courage" and "bravery" interchangeably, but to me they are quite different. Bravery is gritting your teeth and getting on with it. It's ignoring the jab of a doctor's needle when getting a shot or not flinching when holding a nail steady for someone else to hammer. We're told to "be brave" when performing on stage for the first time, changing schools, moving to a new place, or going on a job interview. In these situations, "Be brave" really just means "Don't let anyone know how terrified you are."

Courage isn't rooted in pretense. Courage comes from a place deep inside you. It wells up and encourages you to do what you know is right—even when there's nothing comfortable about it. It's having that hard conversation you've been avoiding, accepting a devastating test result with dignity, and standing up for others when everyone else is sitting down. Courage doesn't replace fear; it allows you to take action in spite of it. So go on, *be courageous.*

Be at Peace
with Yourself

So this is it, the last page. When I started this book, the very heart of it was to connect less with *doing* (lists, goals, achievements) and more with *being* (character, values, tending to your soul). But even focusing on "being" comes with risks. You can still beat yourself up for not being kind enough, present enough, or open-minded enough.

If you take away anything from this book, I hope it's this: you're already enough. You can already live at peace with yourself, regardless of which stage you're at in your life journey. You can breathe deep. You can relax. You can sleep at ease. Because you've already arrived. You're already magical. You're a miracle, exactly how you are today. You don't need to analyze yourself to the umpteenth degree; you don't need to have it all worked out—your scars healed and imperfections concealed. Because they're not really scars and imperfections—they're you. And that's enough.

You. Are. Enough.

It's time to put all the lists away and finally, beautifully, gracefully... *be at peace with yourself.*